before you go:
an Offering

By: Sharon Bridgforth

"Both on the page and in her presence, Sharon Bridgforth is magic. Through reflecting on/illuminating her direct family lineage, *before you go: an Offering* offers the rest of us means to transform our unwitnessed/unacknowledged sorrow, shame, and desire to be loved. With a multitude of ways in—the body, the breath, our own words by hand and through voice—we can find joy as we witness Sharon traveling the road of life behind her mother and in front of her descendants. By choosing to look at the tender places, Sharon has cultivated ways to find beauty and capacity in the truths we learn about ourselves and those we often hold responsible for how we turn out/into who we are. This work invites us to release old stories/knowings we've walked with. In inviting us to open to everything offered to us, including the messy, Sharon welcomes us to the crossroad we have inherited and invites us to choose again/a different way."

— Miré Regulus, *Artist, Community Connector & Co-founder of Poetry for People*

"I experienced tears streaming down my cheeks, cracked-open laughter, and a wildly expanding heart while reading this book. *before you go: an Offering* is a luminous offering—part poetry, part memory, part prayer, and part meditation—on what it means to love through time, across lineages, and while holding the pain and possibility of healing our deepest wounds. With fierce tenderness and holy invocations, Sharon Bridgforth invites us into the sacred terrain of mourning, spirit, and courageous introspection. This work doesn't just tell a story—it opens a portal. A portal to our own capacity for transformation and Love—if and when we choose to walk toward it. I know that I will be walking with this book for a long, long time."

—Erin Walsh, *Co-founder of Spark & Stitch Institute, author, and speaker*

"Anticipating or grieving the loss of a parent can be overwhelming. This book offers a map for the soul through the complex process of forgiveness and acceptance that is possible when our elders are at the end of their life. Part memoir, part guidebook, this work invites you to engage with your grief, one page, one prompt, one memory, one queer prayer at a time. Sharon's courageous introspection and honest naming of difficult truths helps us see that our hardships can be our teachers and our pain can open us up to infinite love."

—Diver Van Avery, *Therapist and Public Artist*

Copyright © 2025 by Sharon Bridgforth

before you go: an Offering is published by Tripwire Harlot Press, LLC.

All rights reserved. No part of this text may be copied, documented or performed without written permission from Sharon Bridgforth. Professionals and amateurs are hereby warned that *before you go: an Offering* is subject to a royalty and is fully protected under the copyright laws of the United States of America, and of all countries covered by the international copyright union, the Pan-American copyright convention, and the universal copyright convention. All rights are strictly reserved. Particular emphasis is laid on the question of readings, permission for which must be secured in writing. All inquiries for amateur and professional performance rights must be addressed to: Sharon Bridgforth at info@sharonbridgforth.com

before you go: an Offering was commissioned and developed with support from the Playwrights' Center McKnight National Residency and Commission Program, Minneapolis 2022 - 2023 and the Playwrights' Center Core Membership 2020 - 2024.

ISBN: 978-1-7341402-9-3 (print)
Dramaturgy and Creative Direction by Jacqueline Goldfinger
Book design and composition by Sheila Callaghan and Daniela Naranjo-Zarate
Cover design by Sheila Callaghan
Photo permission and credits by Sharon Bridgforth and Jeremy Tauriac (pg166)

EXCERPT/READINGS

THE STOOL: Audacious Artist Series The Lorraine Hansberry Initiative at Pillsbury House + Theatre, MLSP. MN August 16 - September 15, 2022.

Playwrights' Center PlayLabs Festival Fellows Showcase MLSP., MN April, 30 2023.

Raising Love & Grief gathering produced by Spark & Stitch Institute and Poetry for People, MLPS, MN January 11, 2025

WELCOME

When I first sat down to write this introduction, I had no idea how challenging it would be to encapsulate something so furiously alive. Two wholly different approaches felt necessary: one to frame the text as a vital break from traditional structures, placing it within a broader artistic and political lineage; the other to meet truth-seekers where they are, with warmth and abandon. I wrote two versions. Together they reflect the book's multiplicity, so I've included them both. Please enjoy this spirited, unequivocally Bridgforthian gesture.

—Sheila Callaghan, May 2025

The Architecture Of Disruption:

What you're holding is a radical experiment in theater-making that defies categorization. In *before you go: an Offering*, Sharon Bridgforth weaves her groundbreaking ritual/jazz aesthetic into a text that functions as performance, self-examination, and creative liberation. It moves beyond tradition in its bold invitation to shape tangible expression from structured confrontations with memory, history, and legacy.

Bridgforth's distinctive cadence pulses throughout, with text that breaks across the page like breath and memories that surface in non-linear waves. With unflinching awareness, she lays bare her struggles with addiction, queerness, health, and family. She then distills these into loving provocations designed for reflection and testimony. Her kinetic prompts translate insight into a kind of gestural unburdening—movement as a pathway to release. What emerges is a tripartite arc that mirrors the cycle of healing itself: naming, probing, and letting go.

In short, *before you go: an Offering* demonstrates how the profound act of bearing witness to our own stories can nourish an artistic practice where vulnerability and intentionality become the building blocks of creation and collaboration. By collapsing the divide between process and product, between healing and holding, Bridgforth urges us to form a spiritual bond with ancestral wisdom and emotional truth. In doing so, she catalyzes collective transformation far beyond the stage, establishing what conventional narrative strives for: a theater of the soul.

Invoking The Divine Unknown:

What you're holding is not just a book. It's a bold, open-handed reckoning. It's not a memoir, yet it's deeply personal. It's not a self-help book, yet it invites profound spiritual transformation. It's not a traditional play or piece of theater, yet it moves with the rhythm and resonance of live performance. It resists categorization. And much like Sharon Bridgforth's body of work, it exists outside of traditional theatre structures. It is theater of the interior—intimate, expansive, personal, porous, and quietly subversive in its clarity.

The text is divided into sections that unfold like portals. Some hold story. Others hold stillness. You may be invited to write in the margins, to say a name aloud, to sit with an old wound, to move your body, or to dream something new into being. Sharon invites you to engage in the sacred labor of reflection and ritual, drawing you into a transformative dialogue between your experiences and the act of creation itself.

In this way, the impact of *before you go: an Offering* becomes clear: it transforms personal inquiry into collective expression, turning each reader's journey through its pages into a kind of art of insights and creative work. Long after you've completed these exercises, you'll hold a tangible testament to the myriad forms of creation and the communal spirit of theater-making—a lasting reflection that continues to inspire and evolve.

For my daughter, Sonja Marie Perryman
the one that Elevated all that is possible for my mother and I.

x

AN OFFERING

This book is queer. It's Southern Spirited, citified and Black. Like me.

Surrendered to the fact that this whole story is told with a shimmy/a tilt/a pause/a flicker/a glimmer/a gesture/a laugh/and a shake . . . this book is Inspired by what I now understand are transgressive tools for thriving that I continue to learn from my elders on all sides of the veil. This how is they Open portals/reach back/push forward-change.

This book is made of prayers, fragile memories, heartache, questions, and conjurings of physical release/in support of Shifting.

Filled with softening and receiving and grieving and loss and fear and shame and feelings of expansive appreciation and wonder . . . this book is made of fragments of what has risen in the last eight years as I have walked with my mother as she stepped into her 80s. As a fall caused her neck to break in two places. As dementia set in. As I have had to look deeply at how I behave in her presence...as I have worked to be who I most want to be when I am with her.

This book is an expression of my Soul calling me to look my mother in her eyes (metaphysically) and say "I Love you. And I know that you Love me."

This book is an expression of my present day understanding of my primary life issue—which is to know that I am Loved—as I look back and move forward in my lived experiences of my life issue's transformation/healing/and release.

Everything that I have ever written, created in performance, facilitated, or poured into mentoring—every bit of getting sober/of supporting my post cancer-cancer free Life/of being a Spiritual Seeker/of waking up to the fact that for the first thirteen years of my daughter's life I was a terrible mother. All of this and more has sourced the excavation and articulation of this/Now.

This book is my Journey with my embodied understanding of my wounded heart. And the work that I have done for my own self/for all generations within and beyond the veil. For my mother. And my daughter. And the soon come.

This book can live as a performance installation filled with audio recordings and live performance and visual imagery and audience participation. It can live as community gatherings curated and tended by artist/healer/activists. It can live as a workshop that I compose live with performers and gatherers.

But what's most important to me, is that this book be an Offering for you. For you reading/holding/walking with this book…I invite you to make this book yours. Fill it with your knowings, your drawings, your dreams, your memories, your flowers, your naming, your conjurations, your rituals. Let this book be your mapping of Love's embrace.

If you chose to turn the page…please know that it is filled with dying, and mourning…and the examination of emotional/mental and Spiritual wounds. There are invitations to uproot and tend your wounds, and to create your own medicines extended from past/present/future lineages. If this isn't the time/if you don't have support-tools-inner resource…please don't go further. At least not now. If you do move forward with this book/please consider identifying your resources, e.g. a Spiritual center, a therapist, AA meetings, a trusted friend, a writing buddy, etc.

There is no right or wrong here.

Follow what is authentically best for you.

I invite you to:
- Write in this book. Journal, draw, paint, pray - respond in whatever way feels most useful to you.
- Honor your intuition.
- Push past your comfort zone.
- Refrain from going to emotional places you can't come back from safely.
- Lean into and cultivate support.

Ask yourself :
What am I feeling?
What is that (the feeling) about?
How does it (the feeling) effect how I live my Life?
These questions, will lead you down many roads of discovery, inspiration, healing, and forward movement.

Please remember/it is okay if you don't do shit.
You might tend to every aspect of this process quickly.
Or you might not ever have the capacity to engage it at all.
Just ask yourself, "am I avoiding - or am I Lovingly giving myself space and time."
Again there is no right or wrong. Just tell yourself the truth.

Notice how you treat yourself.
Be kind. And patient. And tender.

Ask yourself, "what wants to happen."

And Breathe

XIV

TABLE OF CONTENTS

Welcome
An essay by Sheila Callaghan...............VII

An Offering...XI

The Landscape of this book....................1

Prelude..3

Circling...5

Cycling..19

Turning Points...................................33

What is the story of that?....................43

Looking Back/Seeing..........................59

Open/Release....................................67

Blessed Be..91

And Still..105

Shifting.. 109

Reaching..115

Listening...121

Grace...135

Forgiveness.....................................145

Love is..153

Prelude/Circling...............................161

Additional Offerings To Walk With.........167

XV

XVI

THE LANDSCAPE OF THIS BOOK

The left justified text is the "Narrator." The Narrator cycles in Soul conversations with Themselves, their mother and their daughter.

> Centered/boxed prompts are invitations for you to respond in writing or by drawing/moving/singing/speaking (etc)

Right justified text are invitations to physically or in your imagination embody release.
To transform Energy. To lean into Ancestral ways of Being Free.
To create your own Conjuring.

For me Conjuring/Release initiates from memories that my heart holds of my elders in motion. Which now feel like instructions on how to be radically/self-determined and free.
It seems to me that laughing/dancing/gesturing while crying/where ways they embodied getting unstuck.
Techniques they used to root in Joy.

Whatever calls you to Conjure/Release whatever feels true and right and good try that.

This book is divided into 14 sections. These are mappings of my story/which I hope function as potential breaks for you. Of course please feel free to follow any order/any way/any grouping of experiences that work for you. There are a few additional prompts at the end of the book to encourage you to keep Circling with the Work.

*Please interpret words like prayer and Blessing etc in the most queerly-expansive true to you/Infinitely Loving Way.

PRELUDE

And now I am going to be a grandmother

and everything that I believe/have Worked for/stumbled into
been pushed towards with Grace

is Affirmed.

CIRCLING

Who would you have been
if you had felt you were Loved from the beginning.
If you had not been left in the arms of Loved ones
who resented having to care for you.

Who would you have been
if you hadn't been so beautiful a girl
feeling ugly
and wrong.

Who would you have been if you had had a chance to name your dreams.
If you had felt you had a chance
if you had felt safe
if you had felt you had enough
if you had known that you were enough
if you had had the space to open your heart fully.

Who would you have been if you had been able to Love yourself.

Perhaps these are the wrong questions.

> Who are you soon to lose?
> What is the truth about this that is hard to let rise?

My mom,
Sonja Annjeanette Bridgforth
1956 (more or less).

Her eyes they thundered
into my half mothered heart
and I woke.

Let it go
she said
put it down
she said

Shine.

And the Light
pierced the Opening
and released her.

In her rising I expanded
as she smiled into me

me.

Who in Spirit is holding/helping/guiding/walking with you in a Blessed way?
What do they want you to Know?
What do you want them to Know?

Recently I have begun to wonder why I don't remember much of the past.
I see in glimmers and wisps…except for a few clear chunks of stories that return hammer down
and repeat.

This one doesn't circulate often but I do remember it clearly…

The mother of one of your childhood friends was visiting Los Angeles.
She begged you to let me stay with her in Memphis while you went to night school after work. You trusted her and you needed help, so you said yes.

I think I was four.

I can feel myself in awe, looking out the window on the train ride.
All those landscapes flowing and rising and changing.

I remember that her house was dark, and that she'd often sit in front of a mirror combing her hair, looking at me through the mirror. Staring me silent.
I remember she was beautiful. I remember that I was afraid of her.

I can still feel the hardness of the church pews she forced me into, and the pain of her pinching my arm if I moved in my seat. Sometimes she'd lock me in a shed outside her house. It was dark in there. I remember that.

Thank goodness, my great-aunts knew that something was wrong, and they came and got me. I don't remember how long I was with her, but I know for sure that my great-aunts and great-uncles, my great-grandparents and my older cousins Loved me. When I look at pictures from that time, I can see that the light left me. And I see that it returned.

The Light returned.
Me with my great-grandfather, Joseph Hadley Black, Sr.
Around 1962, in Memphis.

What does your future self want your past self to know that will help you now?

I remember that you came to Memphis, I think to bring me back home to L.A. and I remember that I was so mad at you for leaving me in the first place that I wouldn't look at you or hug you. I think I was seven. I remember feeling gentleness, and patience from your response. You let me be in my feelings, til slowly, the hardness in me melted and I was elated to be with you again.

After that, until I became a teenager, I spent most summers in Memphis.
I loved being in Memphis.

I started drinking when I was ten.
In Memphis.

conjure/release

Sprinkle
twinkle
giggle
twirl

dance
run
laugh
play

wonder
delight
look
See

Open
pause
Shine.

Remember

this is how you pray

CREATE YOUR CONJURE/RELEASE

What can you find - through memory/research/or imagining

that can serve as an Ancestral (blood or extended/and claimed) tool

that will help you

reach back/and root in Love?

CYCLING

There are things that I have been holding onto and chewing on and repeating and hurling about, that I have worked through, but am still carrying. Like the moment I gave up on you ever showing up for me. Or hugging me. Or truly seeing me.
I was in the ninth grade. I played sports and invited you to come see me play, and you said you couldn't. Again. In retrospect, as a single parent, you worked a lot of hours to support me.
And still

I stopped inviting you to things.

I slowly drowned in the flooding of this—and in all the ways my years of numbing and running and shame and sorrow and hurt and anger and fear festered in my bones. I became mean and unavailable and selfish.

That is not your fault.

I kept lifting and carrying boulders placed on me
and I walked with them
and added to their weight

until I broke.

> What is the story that you are walking with
> that has a hold on you
> that it is time to release?

The first time I recall feeling conflict with my gender was when I was a small child running shirtless in the sun with my boy cousins at a backyard party. "Put your shirt on," the women whispered, refusing to explain why. The second time, I think I was eight. I was happily day dreaming, looking through a Sears & Roebuck catalogue, selecting my favorite short sets. Suddenly, quietly, I realized that I'd never get those cute short sets, not because we couldn't afford them (which was true), but because the ones I'd selected were for boys. The third time was when the neighborhood boys stopped letting me play football with them because I was a "girl." Over and over, repeatedly, in big ways, and in everyday small ways, I was reminded that something about the way I was a girl was wrong. Each time family members suggested that I "put on a dress," I felt my wrongness, because I hated the way dresses made me feel. I felt my wrongness when I realized that I would never be boy crazy like most girls seemed to be. I felt my wrongness in the fascination I felt for pretty women (especially your friends). I felt my wrongness in noticing that no one ever told me I looked nice. My hurt eventually surfaced as anger.

I now know I had sissy uncles and mannish aunties and a lot of my friends in high school were gay - but I had no way to name their queerness/or mine—in the post Migration era that I came of age in. So as I grew from a tomboy into my many gendered woman loving self …with no language - no discernible mirrors/or support around who I was and how I felt in my body. Being me simply felt wrong. And the disapproval and disgust that was projected onto me, pierced it's way in, and ate me up from the inside out.

What do you see when you look in the mirror?

The way you treated me when I told you that I was gay was the final fracture that severed my willingness to be patient with you. I was in my twenties. I was divorced. My ex-husband and I were born again Christians and thought we were supposed to get married so we did, but as soon as I found out I was pregnant I knew that I had to start telling myself the truth about who I was, and what my dreams were…so finally I articulated to myself that I was attracted to women. And that I wanted to be a writer.

My daughter was a baby when we got divorced. I got on welfare, went back to college and completed my bachelors degree. Her father and I and his family Loved her enough to figure out how to stay connected and support her/and each other, together.

Eventually found myself at The Catch (an iconic Black queer club in L.A.) and everything swirled into place in my queer bodied - woman Loving Spirit.

Something my little girl said to you one day prompted you to call me and ask if I was "a homosexual." It had not occurred to me that I needed to come out to you because I had always been so very queer, that even though I had just found words to name this fact for myself, I honestly could not imagine that you did not already know. So I was unceremonious in my yes, and I was angry. I felt insulted and unseen. Again. You became insistent that I do something—including hormone therapy—to "fix" my queerness. I knew that you felt ashamed of both of us. That you thought you had done something wrong that made me turn out this "way."

I welcomed you in my daughter's life, but I estranged myself from you.

I wish I had been kinder

and more patient.

There was so much wounding

and Joy and beauty

and Blessings and heartache and laughter and distress and awe.

And you protected me fiercely.

It was all so complicated.

Much more than I could understand.

> What are your boulders?
> What boulders were placed on you that you continue to carry?
> What weight have you added to the boulders you carry?

The hardest thing

the thing that returns and haunts me
that I can't seem to heal or shake
is not anything you did.

It is how I treated my daughter.

conjure/release

Pause.

Smile at the weeds bursting the concrete open.
Tilt and listen for birds.
Blink and see the butterflies and bees.

Look Up.
Take one step at a time

breathe

CREATE YOUR CONJURE/RELEASE

What is nature Offering you right now

everyday/in big and small ways

that you can take in

as healing medicine?

TURNING POINTS

> Who Loves you?
> Who do you Love?
> What can you do to Love more?
> What can you do to Receive Love more?

4-7-82 Only seven weeks away? (so they say). We are both very excited. I think you're a girl - if so your name will be "Jasmine JeNette" JeNette after my mother's middle name Annjeanette. My mother and I have a very special relationship. We grew up together. When she had me she was 20, naive, young and alone but we made it. She went to night school, learned a trade and did the things she thought best for us. The two most important things she gave me was were independence and the will to make it and I pray that I pass this on to you for they are essential in this world. I'm not afraid because I know that I can make it. It seems like only yesterday I was leaving home for the first time trying to decide what to do with myself. Though I didn't figure it out then I learned a lot about myself. We all g reach that point when we must break away from

I was about 7 months pregnant when I wrote this in my journal.

My daughter,
Sonja Marie Perryman and I
(in 1983, more or less) in Los Angeles.

By the time you were seven I had been drinking for twenty one years. We were living in Austin, Texas. I was functional. I had a job I Loved. I had great friends. I was on a good path. But my thinking was poisonous. It became utterly impossible for me to make good decisions. I was short tempered and harsh.

I doused your Light.

Your dad knew you were unhappy. He came to visit. He and I and little girl you had a talk, during which (in my remembering) he said, that you weren't happy living with me and that it might be best if you went to live with him (this is not your memory of the conversation). I knew in my heart that he was right. But I was furious. And I unleashed my fury in front of you, and in some ways on you.

Some say we should live without regrets, but I regret that day. I regret everything about it. Except, ironically, that day became a Divine turning point for me and therefor for you. And for your grandmother.

You left that day… to go live with your father. The utter despair that I felt that day and for a long time after/moved me towards healing. To sobriety.

To doing the Soul Work that Shifted Open possibilities for Us.

I have been sober since 1995.

From my journal notes written in the early 2000's (more or less).

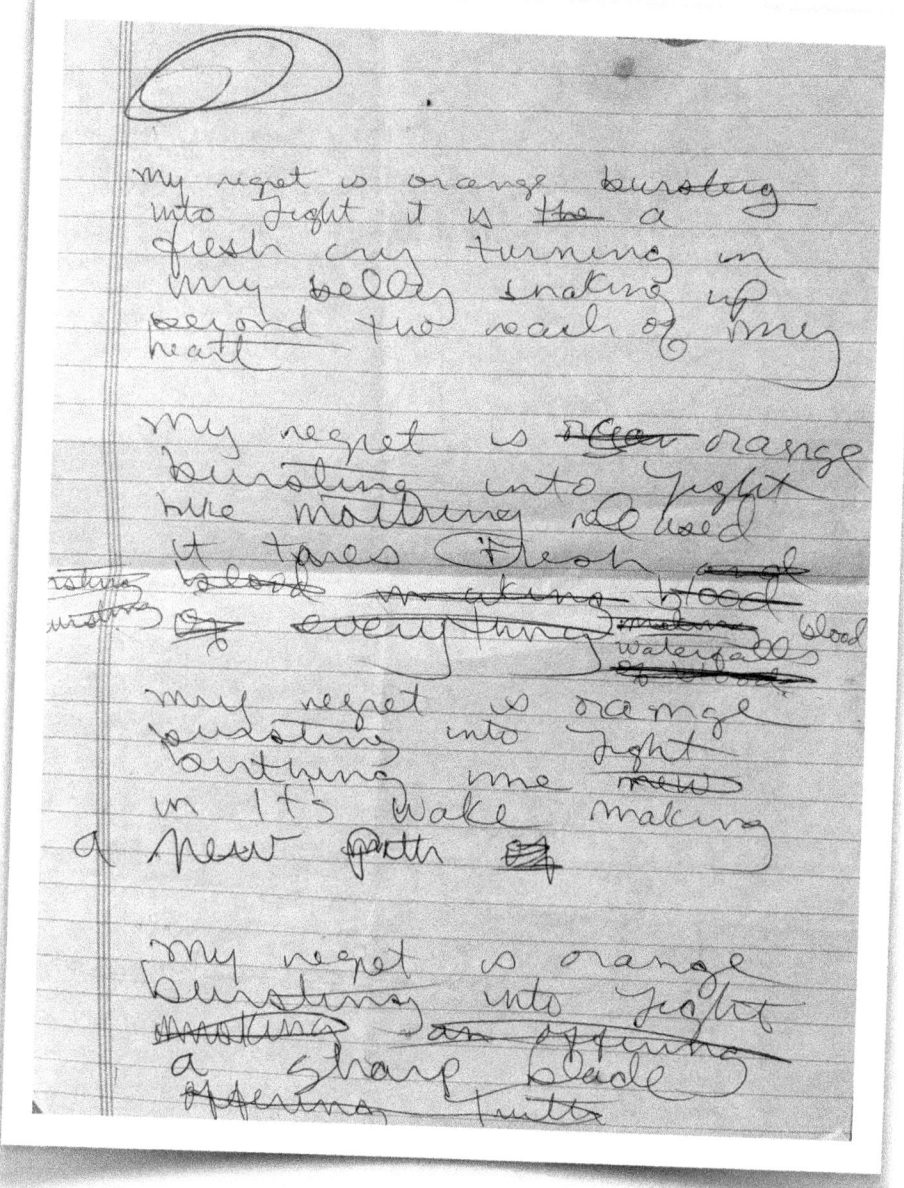

Regret
fear
anger
shame
where do they live in your body?
What are the stories that hook them there?
Which one anchors the others?

conjure/release

Lay it down.
Pour all your shouts out on it

the never felt ones
the ones crooking your bones
the ones buried in your blood
the imposed ones
the inherited ones
the unblessed and shattered ones
the stuffed down the stifled ones
the quiet ones

release them.

After you wake
shake your shoulders
and dance

CREATE YOUR CONJURE/RELEASE

What will help you remove the boulders

the old stories

the weight of things that you carry

that are not serving you?

WHAT IS THE STORY OF THAT?

In my mid-twenties, I developed a pattern of choosing women that could not love me. Beautiful, sexy, smart, hard working, unavailable women. I nursed a broken heart continuously, and passionately, because you see, these women served to prove what I most believed, which was that I was not Loved. And even though in those days, I blamed my girlfriends for my heart break. The truth is, my heart had never - as far back as I can remember NOT been broken. And since I had never tended my broken heart it took me a long time to realize that
I was unavailable to Love.
And that choosing unavailable women
served me.

> What is your biggest life issue?
> What is the story of that?
> How does living with this issue show up?
> How does it serve you?

That picture

your smile

Touches the sad in me.

The knowing of what wasn't to be.

I see you

strong and bent

laughing not reaching

kneeling not believing

in that picture/in your eyes

I see the abandoned places

your yearnings

your fears

And yet you are here

I see you.

And I know even though you couldn't say it

even though you dared not claim it
you dreamt
you made a new way

and you Loved.

So
I stand here
with all that you worked for
all that you prayed for me

and I am free.
I See you

and I Love you.

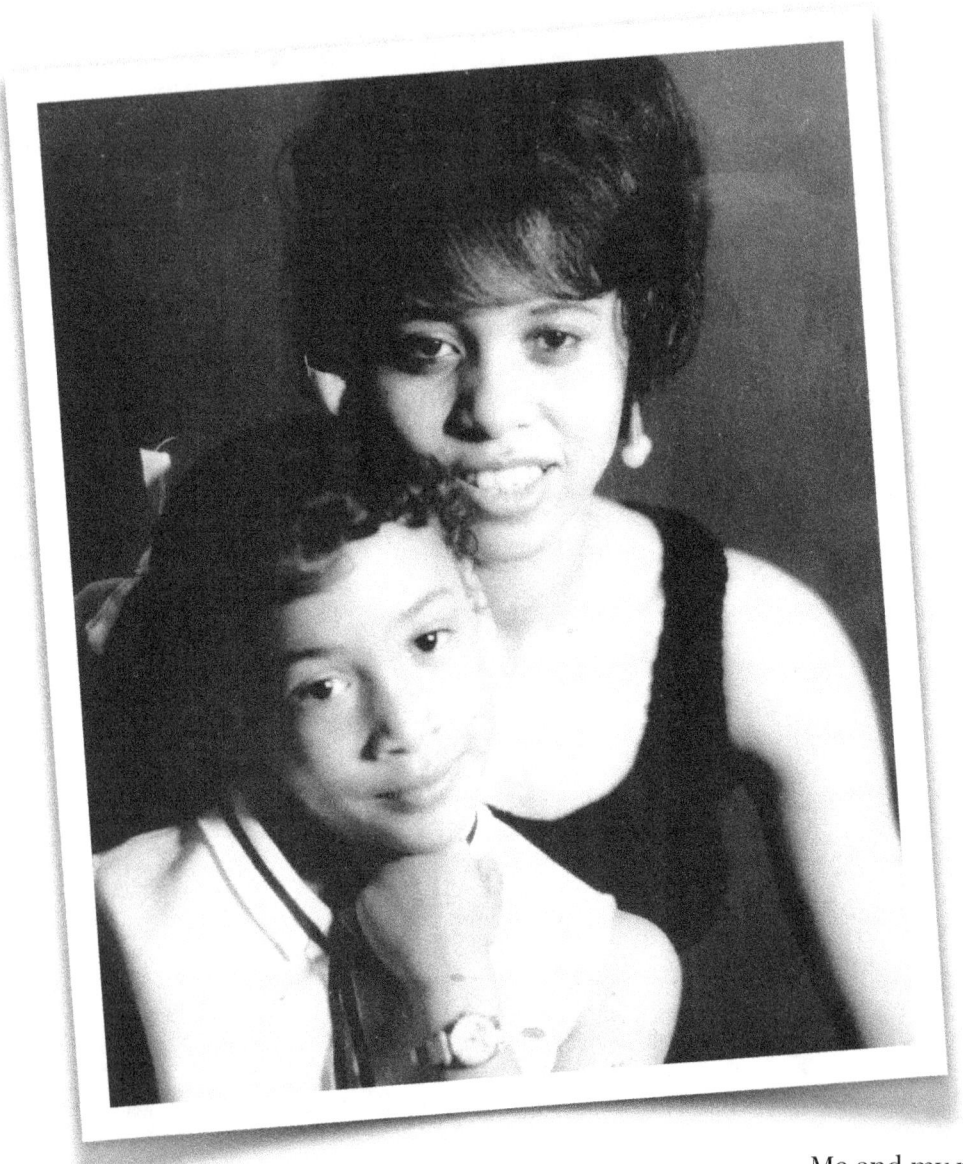

Me and my mom, 1966 (more or less)

I have so many fond memories of being in the back seat
of one of your boyfriend's cars
you in the front
the radio on A.M.
I Heard It Through the Grapevine, Funky Broadway, Mustang Sally, Respect,
Don't Mess With Bill, Sunny, It Takes Two, You Keep Me Hanging On
us all finger popping and smiling and looking good
riding round our neighborhood

slow.

> Who would you like to forgive?
> What is the story of that?

If I could fix it I would.
If I could change it
it would be done.
If I could undo your inability to believe
that you are deserving of Love

I would.

When you were eighty one years old
you fell and broke your neck in two places.
You said you bent down to pick something up and when you rose
you hit your head on the edge of the cabinet.
There was no evidence of that.
No wound. No bruise on your head.

I think you were drunk and you fell.

You have been drinking a lot for as a long as I can remember.

Thank goodness my step-dad heard you calling for help.
And thank goodness your doctor and his staff
listened to me when I said ignore the fact that you were saying you were okay
and please see you immediately.

I was out of town. I was able to get home quickly.

It's a much longer story than this.

But basically
I thought you were going to die.

The only thing I knew to do with all that made me feel
was write

but my words were drowning in my fear of loosing you.
I could only bear what rose in bits.
And only sometimes.

I have been trying to write this for a long time.

Can you read my silence?

You are my longest relationship
the most complicated by far.
You are the hardest to Love.
You are one of the ones I Love the most.

I can't imagine you not being here.
Your laughter
all the ways you boss me around
and irritate me.

I have taken you for granted
walking with you
as if you'd always be here.

Who am I without you.

> What would you have to do to Love anyway?
> What is the story of that?

conjure/release

Stand tall
drop down
swirl

shake your shoulders
smile deep
throw your head back
laugh from your belly
shimmy

release

repeat

repeat

repeat

CREATE YOUR
CONJURE/RELEASE

How can you drop into/and invite Joy?

Even if you can't feel it.

LOOKING BACK / SEEING

Carrying the weight
of living with not enough
and you being so afraid
and me feeling you being
so afraid

broke us.
So much so
that when I look at you now
all these years later
as we sit in the midst of
having a lot

my lens is so cracked

I can barely see you.

I think that after years
of being pushed away.

Cared for but not nurtured

feeling unseen and unsupported

holding your fear in my bones

my Love ruptured and became a streaming pit of aches

fermenting my underdeveloped impulses

drowning me in sorrow.

Not feeling not naming not showing up

not seeing not understanding

not being held not understanding why

I ripped and ran

I drank

I stayed away

I blamed you

I found soft places to land in other peoples homes.

I rotted

Looking back now I see myself
and I say

but that wasn't the whole story.

What do you want to say to your child self that might heal, release and relieve the suffering the younger you is holding?

With shoulders bouncing

fingers popping

head thrown back

hips shaking

and wide open smiles

you danced

Opened by

Aretha, BB, Motown and dem.

The eagle fly on Friday

Saturday nights

we free.

conjure/release

walk around the table three times
take in the smells
See who is there

say thank you

invite delight

now move

CREATE YOUR
CONJURE/RELEASE

What clearing ritual can you Offer yourself

that will help move and Opens portals

Divinely?

OPEN / RELEASE

> What is your cry song?
> The song that makes your feelings rise and wail.

I may not ever be able to listen to Aretha again.
Her voice holds precious memories of us
and how we survived.

I am afraid that if I crack myself open
in the places Aretha's voice pierces

I will fall permanently
away.

I am grateful that a fighting Spirit was modeled for me, because it helped me to survive. But the fight did take its toll on me, and on my relationships. I blamed you for not Loving me, for not accepting me, for not showing up for me. Though I had plenty to feel righteously upset about, the shape of it blew up to mythic proportions. "My mother doesn't Love me," became the myth that ran my life. From that place, I picked partners who were unavailable to love me in various ways. Subconsciously, I cycled around this issue as if to prove to myself that I was unlovable. I nurtured a deep sense of self-loathing. I lashed out at people. I was fighting all the time, even with people that were genuinely trying to Love me or help me. I couldn't receive the good that was right before me, because I was too attached to proving the bad. I am still working through feelings of wrongness. Like when I look in the mirror and think my body doesn't look right. Too many curves. Too womanish to suit how I feel myself to be. I wish someone had affirmed a long time ago that being me, the way that I am, is right. Finally, slowly, with help, I am discovering how to dress myself in the way that I feel. How to have my outside reflect my inside. I am actually looking in the mirror, and smiling. I feel a sense of lightness and joy in my relationships. I've released the need for unrequited Love in all areas of my life.

For more than 22 years, I have been in a Life-partnership that is joyful, healthy, fun, sexy, supportive, loving, and mutual. We have Worked to make it so (but that's a whole nuta story/yeah. One that we are currently working on telling). Her daughter, Leigh was eight when we first met, and twenty when we got together. Leigh is a full fledged/Joyously Divine/Inspiring Blessing in my life. The all of this shines Light on the truth—that Love Is.

My Omi/my wife

She walks like she's got business.
She enters the room bracelets clicking.
She reaches back and carries forward/Black cultures and Black feminist traditions.
She is sweet and spicy.
She makes our home beautiful.
She Loves birds and Rivers and Trees.
She Loves Osun.
She dances until the party is over, laughing from the inside out the whole time.
She WOBBLES BAYBAY.

She processes. A lot.

She asks me scheduling and logistical questions throughout the day as if I can remember all of it.

She snarls at me when I impose help during her struggles with technology.

She engages me in her outfit decision making process/daily. This includes modeling and mirror work.

She is willing to have a dog, because I need one.

She is my protector.

She spoils me.

She Loves my body.

She stands in front of me and twerks and twirls and drops it like it hot at unexpected times throughout the day.

She supplies me with stone jewelry bling.

She binge watches cooking shows with me because she knows I'm too sensitive to watch most things on tv.

She rubs my head at night to sooth my nerves.

She Loves me no matter what. But she says we will only stay married as long as it's right.

She helps me care for my parents/and they adore her. Her daughter is my daughter and my daughter is her daughter and our daughters have partners that we LOVE and together we make family fiercely.

> What Dreams do you have that feel impossible to manifest?
> What is the story of that?

A couple of times a week you call my Omi
and ask her to bring you a bottle of wine.

What you don't know is that the wine Omi gives you
does not have alcohol in it.

LAWD if you ever find out about that
we will all need to run and hide.

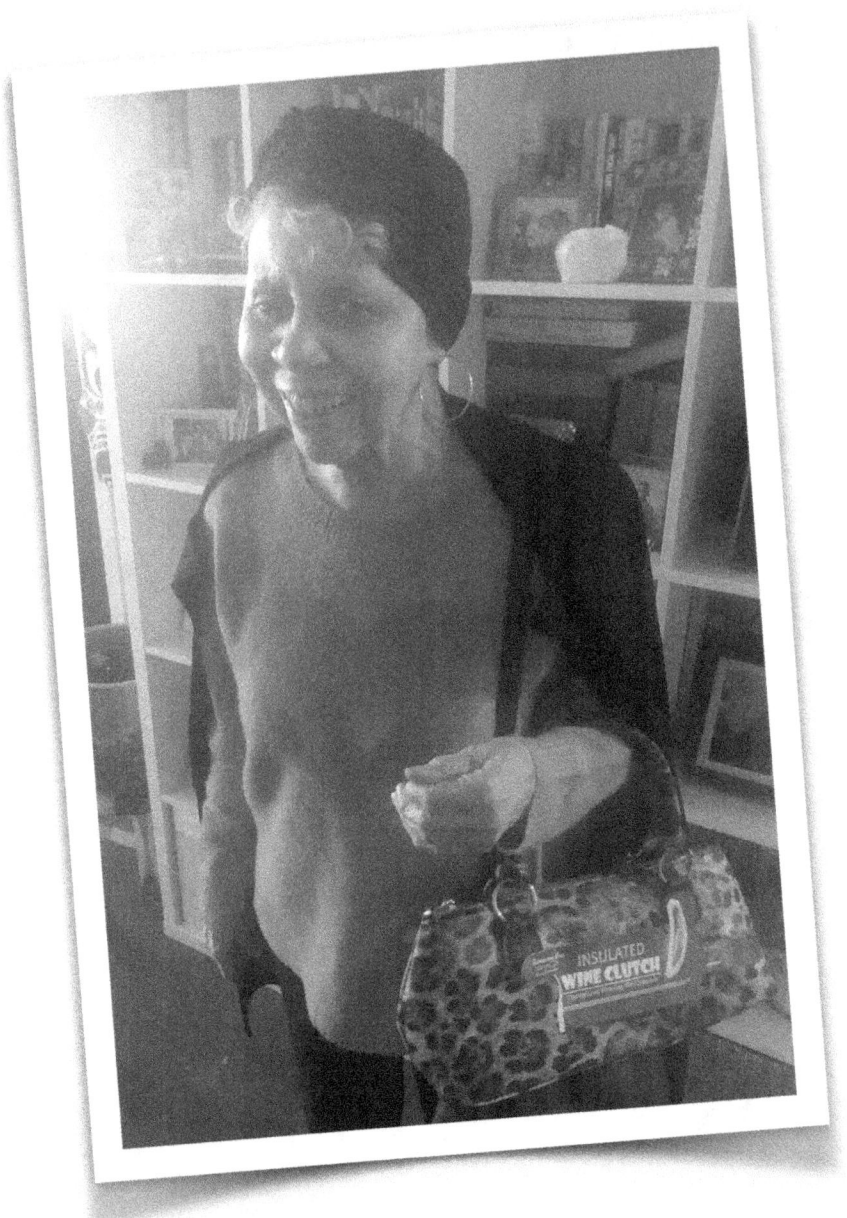

My mom on 12/25/2023 holding an insulated wine purse that my daughter gave her for Christmas.

Determined to be Loving and kind and present when I am with you
I created/and now apply my rules:

- have a car when you visit
- don't stay too long
- you'll never win a fight/so don't fight
- provoke laughter
- give compliments
- when driving her around, put her "boyfriend" (Bruno Mars) on
- if she don't think it's cute, she ain't wearing it
- remember she Loves you
- remember you Love her.

Sometimes I can do this
and sometimes I can't
but more times than before
I am who I most want to be
when I am with you

and it seems that gives you space
to be who you most wants to be
when you are with me.

> Thinking of boundaries that can help you create best practices for you to care for yourself/while choosing to show up for a Loved one, someone that feels difficult to be present with. What are your rules?

I am so much like you

flitting about

never still for too long

cleaning and fixing and adjusting things

double checking the locks and doors and windows

when did that happen.

Doing the four corners
always makes me
laugh out loud happy.

In 2005 I was diagnosed with cervical cancer.
As a gender queer person this was terrifying in a particular way.
One of the many things that I had to battle was feeling violated
each of the many times that I had to lay back with my feet in stirrups.

Thankfully, I had been sober for 10 years by then. It feels like it took years to get the liquor out my organs, and YEARS to even begin to learn how to fully feel and articulate my feelings and to behave in ways that I aspire to. Because of course what I had been doing all along was self-medicating/in order to not feel.
Anyways
I had a lot of support. my Loving-available partner-Omi, supportive blood and extended family, and community. It just so happened that I had great health insurance during that time and I had a fantastic oncologist.

What I remember most clearly from the whole experience
is laying on an exam table thinking *I really want to live.*
And feeling many things dissolve in that moment.
Things that I had previously felt were pressing/important/deep
no longer mattered. I promised myself that on the other side of surgery
I would commit to living fully.

After a radical hysterectomy, and about a year of re-energizing,

I began the Work of honoring my promise to myself.

I started with two questions:

Metaphysically/what must I do to never have cancer again.

And, what does living fully look like.

The answer to both questions was/is

Love.

This led me right on into what they call "the dark night of the soul"

because I knew that I could not fully embody Love

and hold resentment towards my parents.

I knew that I could not fully embody Love

and blame others/for feeling unloved.

I knew that I could not fully embody Love

and not Love myself.

I knew that I needed to let go of everything toxic around how I Loved.

I knew that I had to figure out how to release
sadness, resentment, shame, anger, blame and fear.
I had to practice being responsible for, and articulate in expressing my feelings.
I had to re-imagine my dreams, my goals, my work, my life.
I needed to expand the container/that is ME.

Around the end of 2008, I came out of that dark night's journey
and that year my oncologist released me from his care.
He said as far as he is concerned, I don't have to worry about cancer returning.
Still/I know that the kind of systemic Shift that I promised myself
is a daily Practice.

I asked myself/what was the metaphysical root of the cancer.
Not that I was blaming myself, or discounting my family, history, hard living, environmental factors (almost everyone on my mom's side of the family/all who grew up in a jim crow segregated neighborhood in Memphis died from cancer). But, as a way of feeling pro-active in preventing the cancer from returning, I wanted to know what toxic wastes I could release from inside-out.

I discovered that even though I had done a lot of work and self-reflection

I was still hurt, I did not know how to fully feel or express my feelings in healthy ways. And that I was still deeply attached to my story of not being Loved.

> What are you holding that is toxic?
> How does this play out in your relationships, work, Life?
> What do you have the opportunity to release that might just save your Life?
> What does living fully look like for you?

You know things.

You feel deeply

you are sensitive

you See things.

You are sweet

you are kind

you burst sometimes

so go head on and cry.

It's okay.

You can be broken

and you can fly.

What is your prayer?

conjure/release

stand up
sit down
breathe

hands on heart
bow your head
with eyes closed
Lift Up

Open
moan
rock

CREATE YOUR CONJURE/RELEASE

What repetitive movement/gesture/imagining

will help healing Flow in your physical body?

BLESSED BE

> Who have you harmed?
> What is the story of that?

I can't seem to shake the regrets that lurk and shout and shiver my heart.

No matter how much sense I make of them

they always come flashing through.

Cutting along the way.

Maybe I should be praying for my own mean ass self to be healed.

I wonder how many generations that would help.

The regret I feel
is piled so high
it is packed so tight
it has been buried so long
it is so deep inside of me

I can't move it
I can't break through it
I can't lift myself out of it.

> It was all turned upside down
> I was her mother
> She was my mother
> She was her grandmother
> No
>
> She is my mother
> I am her mother
> She is her grandmother
>
> I think we may have been sisters once

From my journal notes written in the early 2000's (more or less).

I knew you'd be a girl.
I knew you'd be an artist.
I knew you were sent to us Divinely.
And yet

I did not know how to take care of you.
I couldn't access Love beyond my wounds.
I did not know how to navigate my old stories.

Feeling neglected and unseen
pushed away and unheard
the blame that I pointed outward
turned in and buried my tender heart in its rot.

All I knew to do was drink.
Keep going.
Push through.
And run.

I did my best

but I was terrible.

I neglected you.

I was distant

numb and reckless.

I exposed you to toxic people

including myself.

Still

I have always Loved you.

And because I have always Loved no one more than you

finally

after crumbling and shattering and slamming into the bottom

over and over again

I found my way up

and eventually

I Shifted.

I released.

I learned.
I grew

I faced you
and told you all I knew to tell.
Most especially that I know I caused you harm
and I am sorry.

Though I carry shards of regret, remorse and shame
that cut and haunt me
every day

Today I can look at you
with my whole tender sweet heart
and See you.

You are magnificent.

You are powerful

Loving

graceful

generous

respectful

gifted

beautiful

kind

and Free.

I know that you choose to walk with me.

Thank you!

I am so grateful.

Blessed Be

Me (in drag::))), my daughter and mom.
We took this in the early 90's in the Fox Hills Mall in Culver City, CA at a photo center.

Go ahead and Know what you Know
even if you don't know why you Know it.

Even when what you Know
feels too big to contain

let the Knowing seep through.
Bask in it
as it moves you
towards the Light
that Is

You.

conjure/release

Breathe

CREATE YOUR
CONJURE/RELEASE

Breathe.

AND STILL

Recently my daughter asked me why can't I extend the same grace and forgiveness that I give to my Mom
to myself

SHIFTING

> What is your response to Love right now?

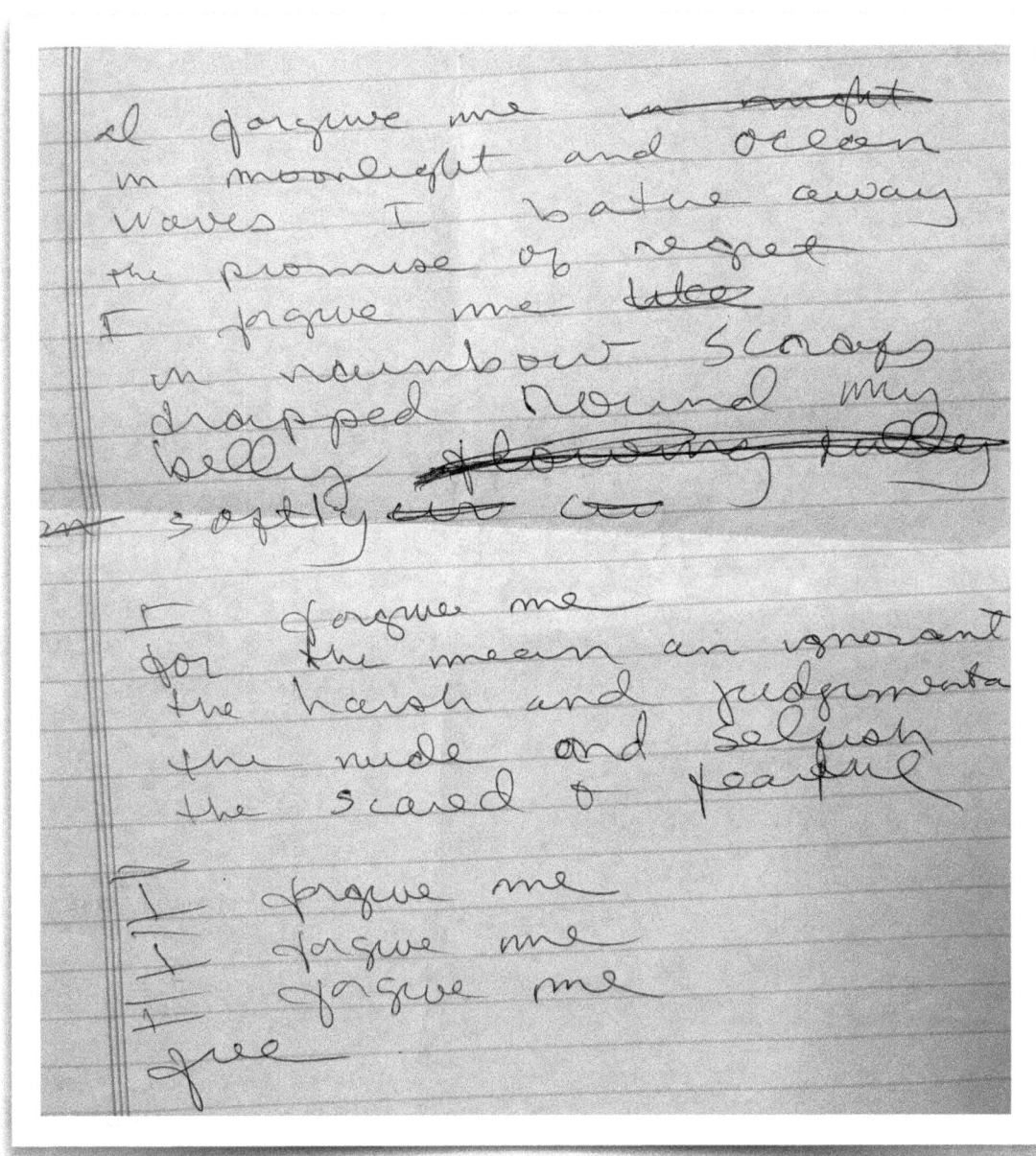

From my journal notes written in the early 2000's (more or less).

conjure/release

point forward
reach back
extend

let possibility move through you

turn swiftly
Shift
turn swiftly
Shift
turn swiftly
Shift

know what you know
fiercely

beckon the way

CREATE YOUR CONJURE/RELEASE

Invite your body to tell you how to

unearth/connect/let go/expand.

Respond to that.

REACHING

Fear stunts us.

Fear that we will never have what we need

that we are not enough

that we aren't Loved.

The truth is

we have always had Love

even when we couldn't feel it

it was always with us

showering Itself around us.

So what I want you to know

what I hope you remember

is the Knowing

that fear is a liar

a trick

a raging joke.

When you feel fear

reach for Love.

"YOUR GRADUATION DAY"

I never told you about that day Sharon, and I don't even know how to describe what I felt. When the march down the aisle started with that beautiful music, and I saw you I started thinking what a long way we came together and how fast time went by. I kept asking, myself is this Sharon? I just couldn't believe it. Then by the time you got to where I was sitting, you don't know how I fought to keep the tears back, I was so proud.

Then at your party later that day, you were just wonderful. When you got ready to leave, you went around to each guest, and there were a lot of people, you told them you have to leave, and you thanked them for coming. You made each one feel they were special to you. There are not many young people like that today.

You are so beautiful inside as well as out, but inside is so important. Please don't ever change! I guess you are tired of reading but tomorrow is not promised to anyone, so I have to let it out today.

"SHARON YOU ARE SOMETHING ELSE"

From my mom, to me. 1975.

> What is being Offered that you are not Fully Receiving?
> What is the story of that?

conjure/release

touch the ground
shout
jump

turn right
shout
jump

turn left
shout
jump

reach up
shout
jump

Shine

CREATE YOUR
CONJURE/RELEASE

How can you instigate Opening

and celebrating?

LISTENING

> What is the Blessing you want to Offer yourself?
> Write it.
> Read it.
> Write another.

When you are able
tend forgiveness.

Start with you.
Forgive yourself.

Practice that.

What is an old wound that you'd like to release?

I have six parents
four siblings
and too many children, cousins, nibblings, great nibblings and chosen family to count.

I am wealthy.

And I am Loved.

> What do you know now
> that took you a long time to understand?

What is your body telling you that it needs?

We are used to
walking with grief.
It's weight varies
it ebbs and shifts
but it is always there
and

we laugh
we dance
we cry
we pray
we commune
we grow
we Love

and we break.

What is your Spirit telling you that It needs?

> What are your Dreams telling you that you need?

Things I've learned from hard to be with Loved Ones:

how to be unflinchingly stubborn

how to root in deep belly laughter

how to give good side eye

how to suck teef

how to dance with Grace.

How to live Joyfully.

How to Love anyway.

conjure/release

give a loud hell no
with a piercing look
and a sharp turn
as you walk away

breathe
stomp
and clear away
the bullshit
the danger
the insults
the ignorance
the put downs
the drama
the muthafukrs

walk away
with your head held high
.
strut

CREATE YOUR
CONJURE/RELEASE

Stir and claim

and stand in your power.

GRACE

If you could see through my eyes
you'd know
how beautiful
how brave
strong
and self-determining you are.

How you saved us.
How you made way for me and my girl
and her One sooncome.

Can you see you through their eyes?

> What is your unearthed Dream?

What do you need?

You are your granny's darling.
The girly girl she always wanted
her mall buddy.
The one she harmonizes with in the car.

You are the beauty she can see
the wonder she holds.
The one…that in her own way
she expresses tenderness to
and delights in.

You are a healer Dear One.

Thank you!

My daughter, Sonja. 2023.

You are made of prayers.
You are Loved beyond the veil.
You've been here before
this time you have more tools.

You are stronger now.
You are healing.
You are a Healer.

Stand fully in that.

Open your Heart

even wider

conjure/release

reach down
drop into your root
pull up the hot
pour the sexy out
to the north
to the south
to the east
to the west
to above and below

reach for fire
unleash your swords
pull all the knives out
shake a tail feather
snarl your face
and be the Glorious warrior
that you are

CREATE YOUR
CONJURE/RELEASE

Initiate yourself in the Grace

and power of all that you are.

FORGIVENESS

Damnit.
I turned all them things that were done to me
that I held onto so tightly
that I so righteous repeatedly talked about
I released all that ugly out on you.

What if you held on to all the wrong I did to you.
What if all you saw when you looked at me
was old stories of hurt and anger swirling round us.

You have every right to pull back
and walk away
to turn and point

but I'm so glad that that is not your way.

I am learning from you
in the depths of our conversations
with every eye to eye connection
all the smiles given

and sweetness extended
the showing up.
The boundaries.

I am learning.

I aspire to rise to your capacity to walk with Grace.

Here is what I have learned from walking with my own hard to be with ass…

The forgiveness you don't give
lives in your bones and guts.
It will leak out slowly over time
and poison the life out of you
and all you Love.

So tend to it.
Knead it out.
Look at it.
Name it.
Let it unravel and make its mess
as you are able.

Over the span of life rolling by
try walking with forgiveness
of yourself and others

see what happens

What would you like to Offer forgiveness to yourself for?

conjure/release

Let the shame out.
All of it that you have ever felt.

The shame that is older than you
the bone breaking shame
the shame buried in your blood
the shame boiling your heart to bits

And after you wake
from passed out tossing
surrendered and washed

rest

CREATE YOUR
CONJURE/RELEASE

Swirl to the surface all that you feel

and all beneath and surrounding your feelings.

Frenzy that.

LOVE IS

This is what it's all been for.

The unearthing of questions
the digging up
and writing through
the Opening/the surrender
the falling out and into
has all been an Offering
gifted to heal me enough
to pray this prayer
with my whole Heart

for my Mother…

May the fear buried in your bones
the emptiness that feeling unloved carved in your heart
and the ways that who you are/and what is possible
was not reflected back to you
be released in all directions of Time
in through and beyond the Veils.

May all the stuck let go and the held on sorrow melt away.

May the sweetness buried/rise and permeate your senses.

May you laugh loud and twirl with songs of Grace

till all the tears you willed away and those you cried

break through

and pave a new road

that carries you to the Light/that is you.

May you finally

Love yourself

enough to Know

that you are Loved.

"A PRAYER OF THANKS"

    You see God, I made this Album as a Christmas gift to Sharon, but I really couldn't in all fairness leave you out.

    I want to "Thank You" for giving me your hand in raising her. You know Sharon and I grew up together so I needed all the help I could get by being so young.

    It's so hard being a parent, and I'm sure I've made some mistakes, but I hope Sharon is as proud of me as I am of her. You know God, when I look back at those years, I just have to say "Thanks". You pulled me through some heavy times.

    I don't think anyone, if they know what all happened, could walk in our home without admiring Sharon and I, all because of you. You know God, these are some trying times to raise children, but when I look at my daughter I know that I have really reached out and touched your guiding hand.

"THANK YOU, THANK YOU, THANK YOU"

AMEN

From my mom, to me. 1975,

I THANK YOU

I THANK YOU

I THANK YOU

I THANK YOU

I thank my Soul for choosing you.

I thank your Soul for choosing me.

I thank all that carried us to here.

As you stand and stay

I call you towards your Opened Roads

turning and twisting and spiraling Light

I call you into the depth of your dreaming

swirling dancing finger popping and laughing loud

I call you inside your praying Soul

flowing and fluid and flowering mightily

I call you to Us
beautiful Blessed and Free
I call you to
Love you
I call you to
to tell you to
that I Love you.

Say Yes
to Spirit
to sweetness
to your Heart's desires
to what you have asked for

say Yes
to you.

conjure/release

Look up.
Ask the Moon your questions.

And in the morning
watch the birds sweep the sky
and the butterflies that linger close by

open your arms and hug a cloud
wave back to the trees
sing with the breeze
witness the bees.

Come to the Water and see my face

CREATE YOUR
CONJURE/RELEASE

Pray.

Whatever that authentically means and Is

for you. Pray now.

PRELUDE/CIRCLING

My dear sweet grandbaby

you are proof that the Divine Is.
That our sacrifices rooted Blessings
and our Dreams manifested Light.

Your Yes to your parents call
Circles goodness within and beyond the veils of time
filling our collective path with wonder and delight.

Your parents will put you first.
They will sacrifice tenderly and care for you sweetly.
They will be wonderful examples of goodness.
And when they fail and falter
like we all do/because no one is perfect
they will re-Align and Open.

You all have chosen each other
and in doing so
you have chosen us.

My dear sweet grandbaby
here is what we want you to know

you are Loved.

Exactly as you are.
No matter what

you are Loved

we prayed you here

and we are with you
always.

Listen for us in the sound of silence
in the movements of hummingbirds and butterflies
in the Flow of wind chimes
the smell of lavender
the salt of the Ocean breeze.

Walk to the Water

put your feet in

breathe

and feel us holding you.

See us in the Moonlight and blazing Sun

laughing and dancing

singing and crying

eating and high fiving

swirling rainbows and twirling colors

gathering/wildly free

self-determined and praying

in praise of the Grace

that Journeyed you through

In this/Now

as you move the portals/Open

bringing all that you've been given

please Know that our great delight
is to Witness you
Being absolutely
authentically
sho nuff you.

We are grateful.

And we are ready

2024. My daughter Sonja, holding her sooncome baby.
Photo Credit: Jeremy Tauriac.

ADDITIONAL OFFERINGS TO WALK WITH...

> Who are you from?
> What have they Offered that you carry?
> How do you honor them?

> What do you believe about time?
> Where does that belief come from?

> What are your people (who are Loving and trustworthy) telling you that you need?

> What healing, what hope, what Light, what Divine change are you Offering your Loved Ones?

> What healing, what hope, what Light, what Divine change are you Offering your communities?

> What healing, what hope, what Light, what Divine change are you Offering the world?

> What healing, what hope, what Light, what Divine change are you Offering yourself?

SPECIAL THANKS

To my LoveBugs: Maria Bauman, Junauda Petrus, Nyx Zierhut, Audrey Hailes, Km Bradford, Katie Ka Vang, Mire Regulus and Karina Maria Muñiz-Pagán for supporting the development process during our The Atlantic Center For The Arts Artist Residency February 11-March 2, 2024.

To: Zola Dee, PaviElle French, Mankwe Ndosi, Katie Ka Vang, Diver Van Avery, Erin Walsh, Mire Regulus, Emma Busch, the Playwrights' Center staff and my Minneapolis family who came to kiki during my April 2024 Playwrights' Center Core Membership workshop.

To: Kayhan Irani, (Amanda) Semente Pereira, Courtney Desiree Morris, Ayana Flewellen for Offering visual Inspiration.

To: Spark & Stitch Institute and Poetry for People for supporting me throughout the long long Journey of birthing this book.

And always to:
My wife
Omi Osun Joni L. Jones
and our family.

THANK YOU!

ABOUT THE AUTHOR

Sharon Bridgforth collaborates with interdisciplinary artists, and audiences to install moving soundscapes of her ritual/jazz texts. Through works that celebrate African-American Southern Migration histories/queerly, she strives to embody the unbending dignity, commitment to community, self-determination and Love of Black cultures that was modeled for her. Sharon has offered art as a vehicle for social justice with organizations, community-based circles and individuals nationally for more than 30 years.

Inducted in the Texas Institute of Letters in 2025, Sharon Bridgforth is a United States Artists Fellow, Winner of Yale's Windham Campbell Prize in Drama, Playwrights' Center Core Member, McKnight National Fellow and a New Dramatists alumnae. A Doris Duke Performing Artist she has received support from Creative Capital, MAP Fund and the National Performance Network. Sharon's *bull-jean & dem/dey back* and *All These Things: A Conversation by Sharon Bridgforth & Daniel Alexander Jones* are published by 53rd State Press. Sharon is an Associate Company Member at Pillsbury House + Theatre (PHT) in Minneapolis, MN. More at sharonbridgforth.com.

tripwireharlot.com

www.ingramcontent.com/pod-product-compliance
Lightning Source LLC
Chambersburg PA
CBHW082208070526
44585CB00020B/2329